A Scorecard Sketchbook for 50 Rounds of Golf

Chris McMullen

A Scorecard Sketchbook for 50 Rounds of Golf

Custom Books

Nonfiction / Sports / Golf

ISBN: 1440417172

EAN-13: 9781440417177

Using this Sketchbook

Cut a scorecard out and bring it to the course or, if you prefer, bring the entire sketchbook.

Sketch the key features of each hole and add draw arrows to represent the strokes that you hit. The long rectangle provides space for the entire hole and the square above it allows for a close-up of putts and greenside shots.

You can place a number next to each arrow to indicate which stroke it is. You can also indicate which club you used for each stroke. Penalties can be noted in writing – e.g. "water," "lost ball," or "OB."

See the sample scorecard provided for a visual example of how you might use this sketchbook.

This pictorial scorecard will serve as a visual memento of your rounds. Compared to a traditional scorecard, the visual detail provided here can help you in various ways. For example, you can use it to:

- recall where the flag was located on a hole-in-one
- remind yourself which club you used to reach a par 5 in two
- see whether you miss more greens right or left, or short or long
- record detailed statistics after a round of golf
- create a yardage guide for a course, showing clubs you've used and putts you've hit before

This is a good companion to other golf books by the same author, including:

- The Golf Stats Log Book
- The End-of-Round Golf Diary
- The Practice Session Golf Diary

SAMPLE

Course: _Dogleg C.C._   Date: _9_ / _4_ / _2008_   Name: _Shorty_

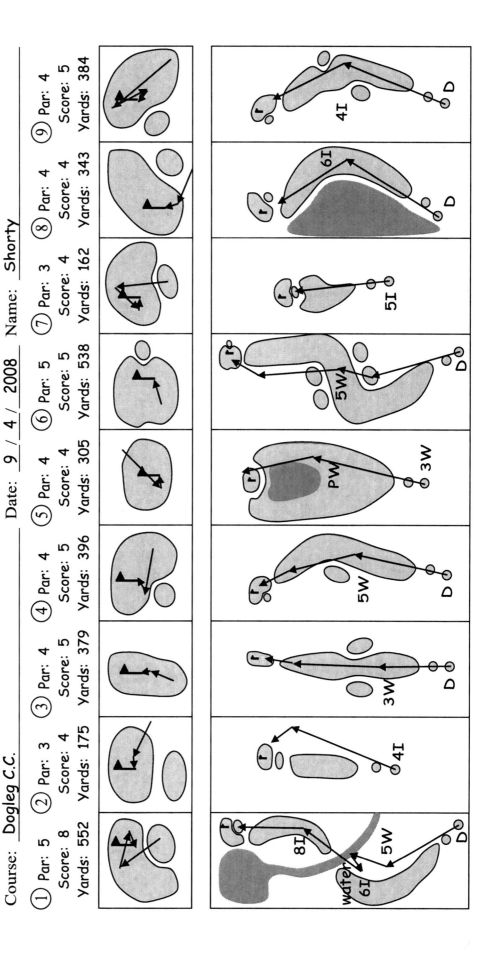

Par: 36 + 36 = 72   Gross: 44 + 43 = 87   Net: 40 + 39 = 79   Putts: 15 + 16 = 31

| ⑩ Par: 5 Score: 8 Yards: 510 | ⑪ Par: 4 Score: 5 Yards: 274 | ⑫ Par: 4 Score: 3 Yards: 345 | ⑬ Par: 4 Score: 6 Yards: 373 | ⑭ Par: 4 Score: 4 Yards: 429 | ⑮ Par: 3 Score: 4 Yards: 138 | ⑯ Par: 4 Score: 4 Yards: 387 | ⑰ Par: 3 Score: 4 Yards: 182 | ⑱ Par: 5 Score: 5 Yards: 544 |

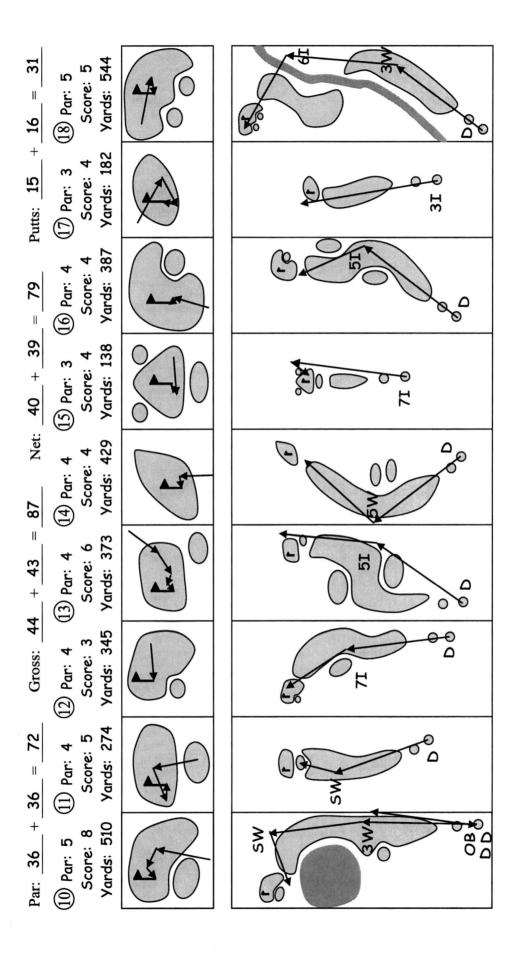

Course: _____

Date: ____ / ____ / ____

Name: _____

① Par: Score: Yards:	② Par: Score: Yards:	③ Par: Score: Yards:	④ Par: Score: Yards:	⑤ Par: Score: Yards:	⑥ Par: Score: Yards:	⑦ Par: Score: Yards:	⑧ Par: Score: Yards:	⑨ Par: Score: Yards:

Par: _____ + _____ = _____   Gross: _____ + _____ = _____   Net: _____ + _____ = _____   Putts: _____ + _____ = _____

⑩ Par:
Score:
Yards:

⑪ Par:
Score:
Yards:

⑫ Par:
Score:
Yards:

⑬ Par:
Score:
Yards:

⑭ Par:
Score:
Yards:

⑮ Par:
Score:
Yards:

⑯ Par:
Score:
Yards:

⑰ Par:
Score:
Yards:

⑱ Par:
Score:
Yards:

Course: _____ Date: ___ / ___ / ___ Name: _____

1. Par:
   Score:
   Yards:

2. Par:
   Score:
   Yards:

3. Par:
   Score:
   Yards:

4. Par:
   Score:
   Yards:

5. Par:
   Score:
   Yards:

6. Par:
   Score:
   Yards:

7. Par:
   Score:
   Yards:

8. Par:
   Score:
   Yards:

9. Par:
   Score:
   Yards:

Par: _____ + _____ = _____   Gross: _____ + _____ = _____   Net: _____ + _____ = _____   Putts: _____ + _____ = _____

⑩ Par: _____
Score: _____
Yards: _____

⑪ Par: _____
Score: _____
Yards: _____

⑫ Par: _____
Score: _____
Yards: _____

⑬ Par: _____
Score: _____
Yards: _____

⑭ Par: _____
Score: _____
Yards: _____

⑮ Par: _____
Score: _____
Yards: _____

⑯ Par: _____
Score: _____
Yards: _____

⑰ Par: _____
Score: _____
Yards: _____

⑱ Par: _____
Score: _____
Yards: _____

Course: _____ Date: ___/___/___ Name: _____

① Par: Score: Yards:	② Par: Score: Yards:	③ Par: Score: Yards:	④ Par: Score: Yards:	⑤ Par: Score: Yards:	⑥ Par: Score: Yards:	⑦ Par: Score: Yards:	⑧ Par: Score: Yards:	⑨ Par: Score: Yards:

Par: _____ + _____ = _____   Gross: _____ + _____ = _____   Net: _____ + _____ = _____   Putts: _____ + _____ = _____

⑩ Par:
Score:
Yards:

⑪ Par:
Score:
Yards:

⑫ Par:
Score:
Yards:

⑬ Par:
Score:
Yards:

⑭ Par:
Score:
Yards:

⑮ Par:
Score:
Yards:

⑯ Par:
Score:
Yards:

⑰ Par:
Score:
Yards:

⑱ Par:
Score:
Yards:

Course: _____   Date: ___/___/___   Name: _____

① Par: _____
Score: _____
Yards: _____

② Par: _____
Score: _____
Yards: _____

③ Par: _____
Score: _____
Yards: _____

④ Par: _____
Score: _____
Yards: _____

⑤ Par: _____
Score: _____
Yards: _____

⑥ Par: _____
Score: _____
Yards: _____

⑦ Par: _____
Score: _____
Yards: _____

⑧ Par: _____
Score: _____
Yards: _____

⑨ Par: _____
Score: _____
Yards: _____

Par: _____ + _____ = _____   Gross: _____ + _____ = _____   Net: _____ + _____ = _____   Putts: _____ + _____ = _____

⑩ Par:
Score:
Yards:

⑪ Par:
Score:
Yards:

⑫ Par:
Score:
Yards:

⑬ Par:
Score:
Yards:

⑭ Par:
Score:
Yards:

⑮ Par:
Score:
Yards:

⑯ Par:
Score:
Yards:

⑰ Par:
Score:
Yards:

⑱ Par:
Score:
Yards:

Course: _____ Date: ___ / ___ / ___ Name: _____

① Par: Score: Yards:	② Par: Score: Yards:	③ Par: Score: Yards:	④ Par: Score: Yards:	⑤ Par: Score: Yards:	⑥ Par: Score: Yards:	⑦ Par: Score: Yards:	⑧ Par: Score: Yards:	⑨ Par: Score: Yards:

Par: _____ + _____ = _____   Gross: _____ + _____ = _____   Net: _____ + _____ = _____   Putts: _____ + _____ = _____

(10) Par:
Score:
Yards:

(11) Par:
Score:
Yards:

(12) Par:
Score:
Yards:

(13) Par:
Score:
Yards:

(14) Par:
Score:
Yards:

(15) Par:
Score:
Yards:

(16) Par:
Score:
Yards:

(17) Par:
Score:
Yards:

(18) Par:
Score:
Yards:

Course: _____ Date: ___ / ___ / ___ Name: _____

① Par: Score: Yards:	② Par: Score: Yards:	③ Par: Score: Yards:	④ Par: Score: Yards:	⑤ Par: Score: Yards:	⑥ Par: Score: Yards:	⑦ Par: Score: Yards:	⑧ Par: Score: Yards:	⑨ Par: Score: Yards:

Par: _____ + _____ = _____   Gross: _____ + _____ = _____   Net: _____ + _____ = _____   Putts: _____ + _____ = _____

⑩ Par:
Score:
Yards:

⑪ Par:
Score:
Yards:

⑫ Par:
Score:
Yards:

⑬ Par:
Score:
Yards:

⑭ Par:
Score:
Yards:

⑮ Par:
Score:
Yards:

⑯ Par:
Score:
Yards:

⑰ Par:
Score:
Yards:

⑱ Par:
Score:
Yards:

Course: _____   Date: ___/___/___   Name: _____

① Par: Score: Yards:	② Par: Score: Yards:	③ Par: Score: Yards:	④ Par: Score: Yards:	⑤ Par: Score: Yards:	⑥ Par: Score: Yards:	⑦ Par: Score: Yards:	⑧ Par: Score: Yards:	⑨ Par: Score: Yards:

Par: _____ + _____ = _____   Gross: _____ + _____ = _____   Net: _____ + _____ = _____   Putts: _____ + _____ = _____

⑩ Par: Score: Yards:	⑪ Par: Score: Yards:	⑫ Par: Score: Yards:	⑬ Par: Score: Yards:	⑭ Par: Score: Yards:	⑮ Par: Score: Yards:	⑯ Par: Score: Yards:	⑰ Par: Score: Yards:	⑱ Par: Score: Yards:

Course: _____

Date: _____ / _____ / _____

Name: _____

① Par:
Score:
Yards:

② Par:
Score:
Yards:

③ Par:
Score:
Yards:

④ Par:
Score:
Yards:

⑤ Par:
Score:
Yards:

⑥ Par:
Score:
Yards:

⑦ Par:
Score:
Yards:

⑧ Par:
Score:
Yards:

⑨ Par:
Score:
Yards:

Par: _____ + _____ = _____   Gross: _____ + _____ = _____   Net: _____ + _____ = _____   Putts: _____ + _____ = _____

⑩ Par:
Score:
Yards:

⑪ Par:
Score:
Yards:

⑫ Par:
Score:
Yards:

⑬ Par:
Score:
Yards:

⑭ Par:
Score:
Yards:

⑮ Par:
Score:
Yards:

⑯ Par:
Score:
Yards:

⑰ Par:
Score:
Yards:

⑱ Par:
Score:
Yards:

Course: _____

Date: ___ / ___ / ___   Name: _____

① Par: Score: Yards:	② Par: Score: Yards:	③ Par: Score: Yards:	④ Par: Score: Yards:	⑤ Par: Score: Yards:	⑥ Par: Score: Yards:	⑦ Par: Score: Yards:	⑧ Par: Score: Yards:	⑨ Par: Score: Yards:

Par: _____ + _____ = _____   Gross: _____ + _____ = _____   Net: _____ + _____ = _____   Putts: _____ + _____ = _____

⑩ Par: _____
Score: _____
Yards: _____

⑪ Par: _____
Score: _____
Yards: _____

⑫ Par: _____
Score: _____
Yards: _____

⑬ Par: _____
Score: _____
Yards: _____

⑭ Par: _____
Score: _____
Yards: _____

⑮ Par: _____
Score: _____
Yards: _____

⑯ Par: _____
Score: _____
Yards: _____

⑰ Par: _____
Score: _____
Yards: _____

⑱ Par: _____
Score: _____
Yards: _____

Course: _____ Date: ___ / ___ / ___ Name: _____

1 Par: Score: Yards:	2 Par: Score: Yards:	3 Par: Score: Yards:	4 Par: Score: Yards:	5 Par: Score: Yards:	6 Par: Score: Yards:	7 Par: Score: Yards:	8 Par: Score: Yards:	9 Par: Score: Yards:

Par: _____ + _____ = _____   Gross: _____ + _____ = _____   Net: _____ + _____ = _____   Putts: _____ + _____ = _____

⑩ Par:
Score:
Yards:

⑪ Par:
Score:
Yards:

⑫ Par:
Score:
Yards:

⑬ Par:
Score:
Yards:

⑭ Par:
Score:
Yards:

⑮ Par:
Score:
Yards:

⑯ Par:
Score:
Yards:

⑰ Par:
Score:
Yards:

⑱ Par:
Score:
Yards:

Course: _____

Date: ___ / ___ / ___

Name: _____

① Par: Score: Yards:	② Par: Score: Yards:	③ Par: Score: Yards:	④ Par: Score: Yards:	⑤ Par: Score: Yards:	⑥ Par: Score: Yards:	⑦ Par: Score: Yards:	⑧ Par: Score: Yards:	⑨ Par: Score: Yards:

Par: _____ + _____ = _____ Gross: _____ + _____ = _____ Net: _____ + _____ = _____ Putts: _____ + _____ = _____

⑩ Par:
Score:
Yards:

⑪ Par:
Score:
Yards:

⑫ Par:
Score:
Yards:

⑬ Par:
Score:
Yards:

⑭ Par:
Score:
Yards:

⑮ Par:
Score:
Yards:

⑯ Par:
Score:
Yards:

⑰ Par:
Score:
Yards:

⑱ Par:
Score:
Yards:

Course: _____

Date: ___ / ___ / ___

Name: _____

① Par:
Score:
Yards:

② Par:
Score:
Yards:

③ Par:
Score:
Yards:

④ Par:
Score:
Yards:

⑤ Par:
Score:
Yards:

⑥ Par:
Score:
Yards:

⑦ Par:
Score:
Yards:

⑧ Par:
Score:
Yards:

⑨ Par:
Score:
Yards:

Par: _____ + _____ = _____   Gross: _____ + _____ = _____   Net: _____ + _____ = _____   Putts: _____ + _____ = _____

⑩ Par: _____
Score: _____
Yards: _____

⑪ Par: _____
Score: _____
Yards: _____

⑫ Par: _____
Score: _____
Yards: _____

⑬ Par: _____
Score: _____
Yards: _____

⑭ Par: _____
Score: _____
Yards: _____

⑮ Par: _____
Score: _____
Yards: _____

⑯ Par: _____
Score: _____
Yards: _____

⑰ Par: _____
Score: _____
Yards: _____

⑱ Par: _____
Score: _____
Yards: _____

Course: _____ Date: ___/___/___ Name: _____

① Par: Score: Yards:	② Par: Score: Yards:	③ Par: Score: Yards:	④ Par: Score: Yards:	⑤ Par: Score: Yards:	⑥ Par: Score: Yards:	⑦ Par: Score: Yards:	⑧ Par: Score: Yards:	⑨ Par: Score: Yards:

Par: _____ + _____ = _____ Gross: _____ + _____ = _____ Net: _____ + _____ = _____ Putts: _____ + _____ = _____

⑩ Par:
Score:
Yards:

⑪ Par:
Score:
Yards:

⑫ Par:
Score:
Yards:

⑬ Par:
Score:
Yards:

⑭ Par:
Score:
Yards:

⑮ Par:
Score:
Yards:

⑯ Par:
Score:
Yards:

⑰ Par:
Score:
Yards:

⑱ Par:
Score:
Yards:

Course: _____   Date: ___ / ___ / ___   Name: _____

① Par:
Score:
Yards:

② Par:
Score:
Yards:

③ Par:
Score:
Yards:

④ Par:
Score:
Yards:

⑤ Par:
Score:
Yards:

⑥ Par:
Score:
Yards:

⑦ Par:
Score:
Yards:

⑧ Par:
Score:
Yards:

⑨ Par:
Score:
Yards:

Par: _____ + _____ = _____ Gross: _____ + _____ = _____ Net: _____ + _____ = _____ Putts: _____ + _____ = _____

⑩ Par:
Score:
Yards:

⑪ Par:
Score:
Yards:

⑫ Par:
Score:
Yards:

⑬ Par:
Score:
Yards:

⑭ Par:
Score:
Yards:

⑮ Par:
Score:
Yards:

⑯ Par:
Score:
Yards:

⑰ Par:
Score:
Yards:

⑱ Par:
Score:
Yards:

Course: _____

Date: _____ / _____ / _____

Name: _____

① Par: Score: Yards:	
② Par: Score: Yards:	
③ Par: Score: Yards:	
④ Par: Score: Yards:	
⑤ Par: Score: Yards:	
⑥ Par: Score: Yards:	
⑦ Par: Score: Yards:	
⑧ Par: Score: Yards:	
⑨ Par: Score: Yards:	

Par: _____ + _____ = _____   Gross: _____ + _____ = _____   Net: _____ + _____ = _____   Putts: _____ + _____ = _____

(10) Par: (11) Par: (12) Par: (13) Par: (14) Par: (15) Par: (16) Par: (17) Par: (18) Par:
Score: Score: Score: Score: Score: Score: Score: Score: Score:
Yards: Yards: Yards: Yards: Yards: Yards: Yards: Yards: Yards:

Course: _____

Date: ___ / ___ / ___

Name: _____

① Par:
   Score:
   Yards:

② Par:
   Score:
   Yards:

③ Par:
   Score:
   Yards:

④ Par:
   Score:
   Yards:

⑤ Par:
   Score:
   Yards:

⑥ Par:
   Score:
   Yards:

⑦ Par:
   Score:
   Yards:

⑧ Par:
   Score:
   Yards:

⑨ Par:
   Score:
   Yards:

Par: ____ + ____ = ____   Gross: ____ + ____ = ____   Net: ____ + ____ = ____   Putts: ____ + ____ = ____

⑩ Par:
Score:
Yards:

⑪ Par:
Score:
Yards:

⑫ Par:
Score:
Yards:

⑬ Par:
Score:
Yards:

⑭ Par:
Score:
Yards:

⑮ Par:
Score:
Yards:

⑯ Par:
Score:
Yards:

⑰ Par:
Score:
Yards:

⑱ Par:
Score:
Yards:

Course: _____ Date: ___ / ___ / ___ Name: _____

① Par: Score: Yards:	② Par: Score: Yards:	③ Par: Score: Yards:	④ Par: Score: Yards:	⑤ Par: Score: Yards:	⑥ Par: Score: Yards:	⑦ Par: Score: Yards:	⑧ Par: Score: Yards:	⑨ Par: Score: Yards:

Par: _____ + _____ = _____ Gross: _____ + _____ = _____ Net: _____ + _____ = _____ Putts: _____ + _____ = _____

⑩ Par:
Score:
Yards:

⑪ Par:
Score:
Yards:

⑫ Par:
Score:
Yards:

⑬ Par:
Score:
Yards:

⑭ Par:
Score:
Yards:

⑮ Par:
Score:
Yards:

⑯ Par:
Score:
Yards:

⑰ Par:
Score:
Yards:

⑱ Par:
Score:
Yards:

Course: _____ Date: ___ / ___ / ___ Name: _____

① Par: Score: Yards:	
② Par: Score: Yards:	
③ Par: Score: Yards:	
④ Par: Score: Yards:	
⑤ Par: Score: Yards:	
⑥ Par: Score: Yards:	
⑦ Par: Score: Yards:	
⑧ Par: Score: Yards:	
⑨ Par: Score: Yards:	

Par: _____ + _____ = _____   Gross: _____ + _____ = _____   Net: _____ + _____ = _____   Putts: _____ + _____ = _____

⑩ Par:
Score:
Yards:

⑪ Par:
Score:
Yards:

⑫ Par:
Score:
Yards:

⑬ Par:
Score:
Yards:

⑭ Par:
Score:
Yards:

⑮ Par:
Score:
Yards:

⑯ Par:
Score:
Yards:

⑰ Par:
Score:
Yards:

⑱ Par:
Score:
Yards:

Course: _____ Date: ___ / ___ / ___ Name: _____

① Par: Score: Yards:	② Par: Score: Yards:	③ Par: Score: Yards:	④ Par: Score: Yards:	⑤ Par: Score: Yards:	⑥ Par: Score: Yards:	⑦ Par: Score: Yards:	⑧ Par: Score: Yards:	⑨ Par: Score: Yards:

Par: _____ + _____ = _____   Gross: _____ + _____ = _____   Net: _____ + _____ = _____   Putts: _____ + _____ = _____

⑩ Par:
Score:
Yards:

⑪ Par:
Score:
Yards:

⑫ Par:
Score:
Yards:

⑬ Par:
Score:
Yards:

⑭ Par:
Score:
Yards:

⑮ Par:
Score:
Yards:

⑯ Par:
Score:
Yards:

⑰ Par:
Score:
Yards:

⑱ Par:
Score:
Yards:

Course: _____

Date: _____ / _____ / _____

Name: _____

	Par: Score: Yards:	Par: Score: Yards:	Par: Score: Yards:	Par: Score: Yards:	Par: Score: Yards:	Par: Score: Yards:	Par: Score: Yards:	Par: Score: Yards:	Par: Score: Yards:
	①	②	③	④	⑤	⑥	⑦	⑧	⑨

Par: _____ + _____ = _____   Gross: _____ + _____ = _____   Net: _____ + _____ = _____   Putts: _____ + _____ = _____

⑩ Par:
Score:
Yards:

⑪ Par:
Score:
Yards:

⑫ Par:
Score:
Yards:

⑬ Par:
Score:
Yards:

⑭ Par:
Score:
Yards:

⑮ Par:
Score:
Yards:

⑯ Par:
Score:
Yards:

⑰ Par:
Score:
Yards:

⑱ Par:
Score:
Yards:

Course: _____   Date: ___ / ___ / ___   Name: _____

① Par: Score: Yards:	② Par: Score: Yards:	③ Par: Score: Yards:	④ Par: Score: Yards:	⑤ Par: Score: Yards:	⑥ Par: Score: Yards:	⑦ Par: Score: Yards:	⑧ Par: Score: Yards:	⑨ Par: Score: Yards:

Par: _____ + _____ = _____   Gross: _____ + _____ = _____   Net: _____ + _____ = _____   Putts: _____ + _____ = _____

⑩ Par: Score: Yards:	⑪ Par: Score: Yards:	⑫ Par: Score: Yards:	⑬ Par: Score: Yards:	⑭ Par: Score: Yards:	⑮ Par: Score: Yards:	⑯ Par: Score: Yards:	⑰ Par: Score: Yards:	⑱ Par: Score: Yards:

Course: _____

Date: ___ / ___ / ___

Name: _____

① Par: Score: Yards:	② Par: Score: Yards:	③ Par: Score: Yards:	④ Par: Score: Yards:	⑤ Par: Score: Yards:	⑥ Par: Score: Yards:	⑦ Par: Score: Yards:	⑧ Par: Score: Yards:	⑨ Par: Score: Yards:

Par: _____ + _____ = _____   Gross: _____ + _____ = _____   Net: _____ + _____ = _____   Putts: _____ + _____ = _____

⑩ Par:
Score:
Yards:

⑪ Par:
Score:
Yards:

⑫ Par:
Score:
Yards:

⑬ Par:
Score:
Yards:

⑭ Par:
Score:
Yards:

⑮ Par:
Score:
Yards:

⑯ Par:
Score:
Yards:

⑰ Par:
Score:
Yards:

⑱ Par:
Score:
Yards:

Course: _____

Date: ___ / ___ / ___

Name: _____

① Par: Score: Yards:	② Par: Score: Yards:	③ Par: Score: Yards:	④ Par: Score: Yards:	⑤ Par: Score: Yards:	⑥ Par: Score: Yards:	⑦ Par: Score: Yards:	⑧ Par: Score: Yards:	⑨ Par: Score: Yards:

Par: _____ + _____ = _____   Gross: _____ + _____ = _____   Net: _____ + _____ = _____   Putts: _____ + _____ = _____

⑩ Par:
Score:
Yards:

⑪ Par:
Score:
Yards:

⑫ Par:
Score:
Yards:

⑬ Par:
Score:
Yards:

⑭ Par:
Score:
Yards:

⑮ Par:
Score:
Yards:

⑯ Par:
Score:
Yards:

⑰ Par:
Score:
Yards:

⑱ Par:
Score:
Yards:

Course: _____

Date: ____ / ____ / ____

Name: _____

① Par:
Score:
Yards:

② Par:
Score:
Yards:

③ Par:
Score:
Yards:

④ Par:
Score:
Yards:

⑤ Par:
Score:
Yards:

⑥ Par:
Score:
Yards:

⑦ Par:
Score:
Yards:

⑧ Par:
Score:
Yards:

⑨ Par:
Score:
Yards:

Par: _____ + _____ = _____ Gross: _____ + _____ = _____ Net: _____ + _____ = _____ Putts: _____ + _____ = _____

⑩ Par:
Score:
Yards:

⑪ Par:
Score:
Yards:

⑫ Par:
Score:
Yards:

⑬ Par:
Score:
Yards:

⑭ Par:
Score:
Yards:

⑮ Par:
Score:
Yards:

⑯ Par:
Score:
Yards:

⑰ Par:
Score:
Yards:

⑱ Par:
Score:
Yards:

Course: _____

Date: ___ / ___ / ___

Name: _____

① Par:
Score:
Yards:

② Par:
Score:
Yards:

③ Par:
Score:
Yards:

④ Par:
Score:
Yards:

⑤ Par:
Score:
Yards:

⑥ Par:
Score:
Yards:

⑦ Par:
Score:
Yards:

⑧ Par:
Score:
Yards:

⑨ Par:
Score:
Yards:

Par: _____ + _____ = _____   Gross: _____ + _____ = _____   Net: _____ + _____ = _____   Putts: _____ + _____ = _____

⑩ Par:
Score:
Yards:

⑪ Par:
Score:
Yards:

⑫ Par:
Score:
Yards:

⑬ Par:
Score:
Yards:

⑭ Par:
Score:
Yards:

⑮ Par:
Score:
Yards:

⑯ Par:
Score:
Yards:

⑰ Par:
Score:
Yards:

⑱ Par:
Score:
Yards:

Course: _____   Date: ___ / ___ / ___   Name: _____

(1) Par:
Score:
Yards:

(2) Par:
Score:
Yards:

(3) Par:
Score:
Yards:

(4) Par:
Score:
Yards:

(5) Par:
Score:
Yards:

(6) Par:
Score:
Yards:

(7) Par:
Score:
Yards:

(8) Par:
Score:
Yards:

(9) Par:
Score:
Yards:

Par: _____ + _____ = _____ Gross: _____ + _____ = _____ Net: _____ + _____ = _____ Putts: _____ + _____ = _____

(10) Par:
Score:
Yards:

(11) Par:
Score:
Yards:

(12) Par:
Score:
Yards:

(13) Par:
Score:
Yards:

(14) Par:
Score:
Yards:

(15) Par:
Score:
Yards:

(16) Par:
Score:
Yards:

(17) Par:
Score:
Yards:

(18) Par:
Score:
Yards:

Course: _____

Date: ____ / ____ / ____

Name: _____

① Par: Score: Yards:	② Par: Score: Yards:	③ Par: Score: Yards:	④ Par: Score: Yards:	⑤ Par: Score: Yards:	⑥ Par: Score: Yards:	⑦ Par: Score: Yards:	⑧ Par: Score: Yards:	⑨ Par: Score: Yards:

Par: _____ + _____ = _____ Gross: _____ + _____ = _____ Net: _____ + _____ = _____ Putts: _____ + _____ = _____

⑩ Par:
Score:
Yards:

⑪ Par:
Score:
Yards:

⑫ Par:
Score:
Yards:

⑬ Par:
Score:
Yards:

⑭ Par:
Score:
Yards:

⑮ Par:
Score:
Yards:

⑯ Par:
Score:
Yards:

⑰ Par:
Score:
Yards:

⑱ Par:
Score:
Yards:

Course: _____ Date: ___ / ___ / ___ Name: _____

① Par:	② Par:	③ Par:	④ Par:	⑤ Par:	⑥ Par:	⑦ Par:	⑧ Par:	⑨ Par:
Score:	Score:	Score:	Score:	Score:	Score:	Score:	Score:	Score:
Yards:	Yards:	Yards:	Yards:	Yards:	Yards:	Yards:	Yards:	Yards:

Par: _____ + _____ = _____   Gross: _____ + _____ = _____   Net: _____ + _____ = _____   Putts: _____ + _____ = _____

⑩ Par:
Score:
Yards:

⑪ Par:
Score:
Yards:

⑫ Par:
Score:
Yards:

⑬ Par:
Score:
Yards:

⑭ Par:
Score:
Yards:

⑮ Par:
Score:
Yards:

⑯ Par:
Score:
Yards:

⑰ Par:
Score:
Yards:

⑱ Par:
Score:
Yards:

Course: _____

Date: ___ / ___ / ___

Name: _____

(1) Par:
Score:
Yards:

(2) Par:
Score:
Yards:

(3) Par:
Score:
Yards:

(4) Par:
Score:
Yards:

(5) Par:
Score:
Yards:

(6) Par:
Score:
Yards:

(7) Par:
Score:
Yards:

(8) Par:
Score:
Yards:

(9) Par:
Score:
Yards:

Par: _____ + _____ = _____   Gross: _____ + _____ = _____   Net: _____ + _____ = _____   Putts: _____ + _____ = _____

⑩ Par:
Score:
Yards:

⑪ Par:
Score:
Yards:

⑫ Par:
Score:
Yards:

⑬ Par:
Score:
Yards:

⑭ Par:
Score:
Yards:

⑮ Par:
Score:
Yards:

⑯ Par:
Score:
Yards:

⑰ Par:
Score:
Yards:

⑱ Par:
Score:
Yards:

Course: _____

Date: ____ / ____ / ____

Name: _____

Hole	Par	Score	Yards
①	Par:	Score:	Yards:
②	Par:	Score:	Yards:
③	Par:	Score:	Yards:
④	Par:	Score:	Yards:
⑤	Par:	Score:	Yards:
⑥	Par:	Score:	Yards:
⑦	Par:	Score:	Yards:
⑧	Par:	Score:	Yards:
⑨	Par:	Score:	Yards:

Par: _____ + _____ = _____   Gross: _____ + _____ = _____   Net: _____ + _____ = _____   Putts: _____ + _____ = _____

⑩ Par:
Score:
Yards:

⑪ Par:
Score:
Yards:

⑫ Par:
Score:
Yards:

⑬ Par:
Score:
Yards:

⑭ Par:
Score:
Yards:

⑮ Par:
Score:
Yards:

⑯ Par:
Score:
Yards:

⑰ Par:
Score:
Yards:

⑱ Par:
Score:
Yards:

Course: _____

Date: ___ / ___ / ___

Name: _____

① Par:
Score:
Yards:

② Par:
Score:
Yards:

③ Par:
Score:
Yards:

④ Par:
Score:
Yards:

⑤ Par:
Score:
Yards:

⑥ Par:
Score:
Yards:

⑦ Par:
Score:
Yards:

⑧ Par:
Score:
Yards:

⑨ Par:
Score:
Yards:

Par: _____ + _____ = _____   Gross: _____ + _____ = _____   Net: _____ + _____ = _____   Putts: _____ + _____ = _____

⑩ Par:
Score:
Yards:

⑪ Par:
Score:
Yards:

⑫ Par:
Score:
Yards:

⑬ Par:
Score:
Yards:

⑭ Par:
Score:
Yards:

⑮ Par:
Score:
Yards:

⑯ Par:
Score:
Yards:

⑰ Par:
Score:
Yards:

⑱ Par:
Score:
Yards:

Course: _____ Date: ___ / ___ / ___ Name: _____

① Par: Score: Yards:	② Par: Score: Yards:	③ Par: Score: Yards:	④ Par: Score: Yards:	⑤ Par: Score: Yards:	⑥ Par: Score: Yards:	⑦ Par: Score: Yards:	⑧ Par: Score: Yards:	⑨ Par: Score: Yards:

Par: _____ + _____ = _____   Gross: _____ + _____ = _____   Net: _____ + _____ = _____   Putts: _____ + _____ = _____

⑩ Par:
Score:
Yards:

⑪ Par:
Score:
Yards:

⑫ Par:
Score:
Yards:

⑬ Par:
Score:
Yards:

⑭ Par:
Score:
Yards:

⑮ Par:
Score:
Yards:

⑯ Par:
Score:
Yards:

⑰ Par:
Score:
Yards:

⑱ Par:
Score:
Yards:

Course: _____

Date: ___ / ___ / ___

Name: _____

① Par:
Score:
Yards:

② Par:
Score:
Yards:

③ Par:
Score:
Yards:

④ Par:
Score:
Yards:

⑤ Par:
Score:
Yards:

⑥ Par:
Score:
Yards:

⑦ Par:
Score:
Yards:

⑧ Par:
Score:
Yards:

⑨ Par:
Score:
Yards:

Par: ____ + ____ = ____   Gross: ____ + ____ = ____   Net: ____ + ____ = ____   Putts: ____ + ____ = ____

⑩ Par:
Score:
Yards:

⑪ Par:
Score:
Yards:

⑫ Par:
Score:
Yards:

⑬ Par:
Score:
Yards:

⑭ Par:
Score:
Yards:

⑮ Par:
Score:
Yards:

⑯ Par:
Score:
Yards:

⑰ Par:
Score:
Yards:

⑱ Par:
Score:
Yards:

Course: _____

Date: ____ / ____ / ____

Name: _____

① Par: Score: Yards:	② Par: Score: Yards:	③ Par: Score: Yards:	④ Par: Score: Yards:	⑤ Par: Score: Yards:	⑥ Par: Score: Yards:	⑦ Par: Score: Yards:	⑧ Par: Score: Yards:	⑨ Par: Score: Yards:

Par: _____ + _____ = _____   Gross: _____   Net: _____ + _____ = _____   Putts: _____ + _____ = _____

⑩ Par: _____
Score: _____
Yards: _____

⑪ Par: _____
Score: _____
Yards: _____

⑫ Par: _____
Score: _____
Yards: _____

⑬ Par: _____
Score: _____
Yards: _____

⑭ Par: _____
Score: _____
Yards: _____

⑮ Par: _____
Score: _____
Yards: _____

⑯ Par: _____
Score: _____
Yards: _____

⑰ Par: _____
Score: _____
Yards: _____

⑱ Par: _____
Score: _____
Yards: _____

Course: _____

Date: ___ / ___ / ___

Name: _____

① Par:
Score:
Yards:

② Par:
Score:
Yards:

③ Par:
Score:
Yards:

④ Par:
Score:
Yards:

⑤ Par:
Score:
Yards:

⑥ Par:
Score:
Yards:

⑦ Par:
Score:
Yards:

⑧ Par:
Score:
Yards:

⑨ Par:
Score:
Yards:

Par: _____ + _____ = _____ Gross: _____ Net: _____ + _____ = _____ Putts: _____ + _____ = _____

⑩ Par:
Score:
Yards:

⑪ Par:
Score:
Yards:

⑫ Par:
Score:
Yards:

⑬ Par:
Score:
Yards:

⑭ Par:
Score:
Yards:

⑮ Par:
Score:
Yards:

⑯ Par:
Score:
Yards:

⑰ Par:
Score:
Yards:

⑱ Par:
Score:
Yards:

Course: _____ Date: ___ / ___ / ___ Name: _____

① Par:
Score:
Yards:

② Par:
Score:
Yards:

③ Par:
Score:
Yards:

④ Par:
Score:
Yards:

⑤ Par:
Score:
Yards:

⑥ Par:
Score:
Yards:

⑦ Par:
Score:
Yards:

⑧ Par:
Score:
Yards:

⑨ Par:
Score:
Yards:

Par: _____ + _____ = _____   Gross: _____ + _____ = _____   Net: _____ + _____ = _____   Putts: _____ + _____ = _____

⑩ Par:
Score:
Yards:

⑪ Par:
Score:
Yards:

⑫ Par:
Score:
Yards:

⑬ Par:
Score:
Yards:

⑭ Par:
Score:
Yards:

⑮ Par:
Score:
Yards:

⑯ Par:
Score:
Yards:

⑰ Par:
Score:
Yards:

⑱ Par:
Score:
Yards:

Course: _____

Date: ___ / ___ / ___

Name: _____

(1) Par: Score: Yards:	(2) Par: Score: Yards:	(3) Par: Score: Yards:	(4) Par: Score: Yards:	(5) Par: Score: Yards:	(6) Par: Score: Yards:	(7) Par: Score: Yards:	(8) Par: Score: Yards:	(9) Par: Score: Yards:

Par: _____ + _____ = _____   Gross: _____ + _____ = _____   Net: _____ + _____ = _____   Putts: _____ + _____ = _____

⑩ Par:
Score:
Yards:

⑪ Par:
Score:
Yards:

⑫ Par:
Score:
Yards:

⑬ Par:
Score:
Yards:

⑭ Par:
Score:
Yards:

⑮ Par:
Score:
Yards:

⑯ Par:
Score:
Yards:

⑰ Par:
Score:
Yards:

⑱ Par:
Score:
Yards:

Course: _____ Date: ____ / ____ / ____ Name: _____

① Par: Score: Yards:	② Par: Score: Yards:	③ Par: Score: Yards:	④ Par: Score: Yards:	⑤ Par: Score: Yards:	⑥ Par: Score: Yards:	⑦ Par: Score: Yards:	⑧ Par: Score: Yards:	⑨ Par: Score: Yards:

Par: _____ + _____ = _____ Gross: _____ + _____ = _____ Net: _____ + _____ = _____ Putts: _____ + _____ = _____

⑩ Par: Score: Yards:	⑪ Par: Score: Yards:	⑫ Par: Score: Yards:	⑬ Par: Score: Yards:	⑭ Par: Score: Yards:	⑮ Par: Score: Yards:	⑯ Par: Score: Yards:	⑰ Par: Score: Yards:	⑱ Par: Score: Yards:

Course: _____

Date: ____ / ____ / ____

Name: _____

① Par: ___ Score: ___ Yards: ___

② Par: ___ Score: ___ Yards: ___

③ Par: ___ Score: ___ Yards: ___

④ Par: ___ Score: ___ Yards: ___

⑤ Par: ___ Score: ___ Yards: ___

⑥ Par: ___ Score: ___ Yards: ___

⑦ Par: ___ Score: ___ Yards: ___

⑧ Par: ___ Score: ___ Yards: ___

⑨ Par: ___ Score: ___ Yards: ___

Par: _____ + _____ = _____   Gross: _____ + _____ = _____   Net: _____ + _____ = _____   Putts: _____ + _____ = _____

⑩ Par:
Score:
Yards:

⑪ Par:
Score:
Yards:

⑫ Par:
Score:
Yards:

⑬ Par:
Score:
Yards:

⑭ Par:
Score:
Yards:

⑮ Par:
Score:
Yards:

⑯ Par:
Score:
Yards:

⑰ Par:
Score:
Yards:

⑱ Par:
Score:
Yards:

Course: _____ Date: ____ / ____ / ____ Name: _____

① Par: Score: Yards:	② Par: Score: Yards:	③ Par: Score: Yards:	④ Par: Score: Yards:	⑤ Par: Score: Yards:	⑥ Par: Score: Yards:	⑦ Par: Score: Yards:	⑧ Par: Score: Yards:	⑨ Par: Score: Yards:

Par: _____ + _____ = _____ Gross: _____ + _____ = _____ Net: _____ + _____ = _____ Putts: _____ + _____ = _____

⑩ Par: Score: Yards:	⑪ Par: Score: Yards:	⑫ Par: Score: Yards:	⑬ Par: Score: Yards:	⑭ Par: Score: Yards:	⑮ Par: Score: Yards:	⑯ Par: Score: Yards:	⑰ Par: Score: Yards:	⑱ Par: Score: Yards:

Course: _____ Date: ___ / ___ / ___ Name: _____

① Par: Score: Yards:	② Par: Score: Yards:	③ Par: Score: Yards:	④ Par: Score: Yards:	⑤ Par: Score: Yards:	⑥ Par: Score: Yards:	⑦ Par: Score: Yards:	⑧ Par: Score: Yards:	⑨ Par: Score: Yards:

Par: _____ + _____ = _____   Gross: _____ + _____ = _____   Net: _____ + _____ = _____   Putts: _____ + _____ = _____

⑩ Par:
Score:
Yards:

⑪ Par:
Score:
Yards:

⑫ Par:
Score:
Yards:

⑬ Par:
Score:
Yards:

⑭ Par:
Score:
Yards:

⑮ Par:
Score:
Yards:

⑯ Par:
Score:
Yards:

⑰ Par:
Score:
Yards:

⑱ Par:
Score:
Yards:

Course: _____ Date: ___ / ___ / ___ Name: _____

1. Par:
   Score:
   Yards:

2. Par:
   Score:
   Yards:

3. Par:
   Score:
   Yards:

4. Par:
   Score:
   Yards:

5. Par:
   Score:
   Yards:

6. Par:
   Score:
   Yards:

7. Par:
   Score:
   Yards:

8. Par:
   Score:
   Yards:

9. Par:
   Score:
   Yards:

Par: _____ + _____ = _____   Gross: _____ + _____ = _____   Net: _____ + _____ = _____   Putts: _____ + _____ = _____

⑩ Par: Score: Yards:	⑪ Par: Score: Yards:	⑫ Par: Score: Yards:	⑬ Par: Score: Yards:	⑭ Par: Score: Yards:	⑮ Par: Score: Yards:	⑯ Par: Score: Yards:	⑰ Par: Score: Yards:	⑱ Par: Score: Yards:

Course: _____

Date: ___ / ___ / ___

Name: _____

① Par: _____
Score: _____
Yards: _____

② Par: _____
Score: _____
Yards: _____

③ Par: _____
Score: _____
Yards: _____

④ Par: _____
Score: _____
Yards: _____

⑤ Par: _____
Score: _____
Yards: _____

⑥ Par: _____
Score: _____
Yards: _____

⑦ Par: _____
Score: _____
Yards: _____

⑧ Par: _____
Score: _____
Yards: _____

⑨ Par: _____
Score: _____
Yards: _____

Par: _____ + _____ = _____   Gross: _____ + _____ = _____   Net: _____ + _____ = _____   Putts: _____ + _____ = _____

⑩ Par: Score: Yards:

⑪ Par: Score: Yards:

⑫ Par: Score: Yards:

⑬ Par: Score: Yards:

⑭ Par: Score: Yards:

⑮ Par: Score: Yards:

⑯ Par: Score: Yards:

⑰ Par: Score: Yards:

⑱ Par: Score: Yards:

Course: _____

Date: ___ / ___ / ___

Name: _____

① Par:
Score:
Yards:

② Par:
Score:
Yards:

③ Par:
Score:
Yards:

④ Par:
Score:
Yards:

⑤ Par:
Score:
Yards:

⑥ Par:
Score:
Yards:

⑦ Par:
Score:
Yards:

⑧ Par:
Score:
Yards:

⑨ Par:
Score:
Yards:

Par: _____ + _____ = _____   Gross: _____ + _____ = _____   Net: _____ + _____ = _____   Putts: _____ + _____ = _____

⑩ Par: Score: Yards:	⑪ Par: Score: Yards:	⑫ Par: Score: Yards:	⑬ Par: Score: Yards:	⑭ Par: Score: Yards:	⑮ Par: Score: Yards:	⑯ Par: Score: Yards:	⑰ Par: Score: Yards:	⑱ Par: Score: Yards:

Course: _____

Date: ___ / ___ / ___ Name: _____

① Par:
Score:
Yards:

② Par:
Score:
Yards:

③ Par:
Score:
Yards:

④ Par:
Score:
Yards:

⑤ Par:
Score:
Yards:

⑥ Par:
Score:
Yards:

⑦ Par:
Score:
Yards:

⑧ Par:
Score:
Yards:

⑨ Par:
Score:
Yards:

Par: _____ + _____ = _____ Gross: _____ + _____ = _____ Net: _____ + _____ = _____ Putts: _____ + _____ =

⑩ Par: _____ Score: _____ Yards: _____

⑪ Par: _____ Score: _____ Yards: _____

⑫ Par: _____ Score: _____ Yards: _____

⑬ Par: _____ Score: _____ Yards: _____

⑭ Par: _____ Score: _____ Yards: _____

⑮ Par: _____ Score: _____ Yards: _____

⑯ Par: _____ Score: _____ Yards: _____

⑰ Par: _____ Score: _____ Yards: _____

⑱ Par: _____ Score: _____ Yards: _____

Course: _____

Date: ____ / ____ / ____

Name: _____

① Par: Score: Yards:	② Par: Score: Yards:	③ Par: Score: Yards:	④ Par: Score: Yards:	⑤ Par: Score: Yards:	⑥ Par: Score: Yards:	⑦ Par: Score: Yards:	⑧ Par: Score: Yards:	⑨ Par: Score: Yards:

Par: _____ + _____ = _____   Gross: _____ + _____ = _____   Net: _____ + _____ = _____   Putts: _____ + _____ = _____

⑩ Par: Score: Yards:	⑪ Par: Score: Yards:	⑫ Par: Score: Yards:	⑬ Par: Score: Yards:	⑭ Par: Score: Yards:	⑮ Par: Score: Yards:	⑯ Par: Score: Yards:	⑰ Par: Score: Yards:	⑱ Par: Score: Yards:

Course: _____ Date: ___ / ___ / ___ Name: _____

① Par: Score: Yards:	② Par: Score: Yards:	③ Par: Score: Yards:	④ Par: Score: Yards:	⑤ Par: Score: Yards:	⑥ Par: Score: Yards:	⑦ Par: Score: Yards:	⑧ Par: Score: Yards:	⑨ Par: Score: Yards:

Par: _____ + _____ = _____   Gross: _____ + _____ = _____   Net: _____ + _____ = _____   Putts: _____ + _____ = _____

⑩ Par: _____   ⑪ Par: _____   ⑫ Par: _____   ⑬ Par: _____   ⑭ Par: _____   ⑮ Par: _____   ⑯ Par: _____   ⑰ Par: _____   ⑱ Par: _____
Score: _____   Score: _____   Score: _____   Score: _____   Score: _____   Score: _____   Score: _____   Score: _____   Score: _____
Yards: _____   Yards: _____   Yards: _____   Yards: _____   Yards: _____   Yards: _____   Yards: _____   Yards: _____   Yards: _____

Course: _____

Date: _____ / _____ / _____

Name: _____

① Par:
Score:
Yards:

② Par:
Score:
Yards:

③ Par:
Score:
Yards:

④ Par:
Score:
Yards:

⑤ Par:
Score:
Yards:

⑥ Par:
Score:
Yards:

⑦ Par:
Score:
Yards:

⑧ Par:
Score:
Yards:

⑨ Par:
Score:
Yards:

Par: _____ + _____ = _____   Gross: _____ + _____ = _____   Net: _____ + _____ = _____   Putts: _____ + _____ = _____

⑩ Par:
Score:
Yards:

⑪ Par:
Score:
Yards:

⑫ Par:
Score:
Yards:

⑬ Par:
Score:
Yards:

⑭ Par:
Score:
Yards:

⑮ Par:
Score:
Yards:

⑯ Par:
Score:
Yards:

⑰ Par:
Score:
Yards:

⑱ Par:
Score:
Yards:

Course: _____

Date: _____ / _____ / _____

Name: _____

(1) Par: Score: Yards:	(2) Par: Score: Yards:	(3) Par: Score: Yards:	(4) Par: Score: Yards:	(5) Par: Score: Yards:	(6) Par: Score: Yards:	(7) Par: Score: Yards:	(8) Par: Score: Yards:	(9) Par: Score: Yards:

Par: _____ + _____ = _____   Gross: _____ + _____ = _____   Net: _____ + _____ = _____   Putts: _____ + _____ = _____

⑩ Par:
Score:
Yards:

⑪ Par:
Score:
Yards:

⑫ Par:
Score:
Yards:

⑬ Par:
Score:
Yards:

⑭ Par:
Score:
Yards:

⑮ Par:
Score:
Yards:

⑯ Par:
Score:
Yards:

⑰ Par:
Score:
Yards:

⑱ Par:
Score:
Yards:

Course: _____   Date: ___ / ___ / ___   Name: _____

① Par: ___ Score: ___ Yards: ___	② Par: ___ Score: ___ Yards: ___	③ Par: ___ Score: ___ Yards: ___	④ Par: ___ Score: ___ Yards: ___	⑤ Par: ___ Score: ___ Yards: ___	⑥ Par: ___ Score: ___ Yards: ___	⑦ Par: ___ Score: ___ Yards: ___	⑧ Par: ___ Score: ___ Yards: ___	⑨ Par: ___ Score: ___ Yards: ___

Par: _____ + _____ = _____ Gross: _____ + _____ = _____ Net: _____ + _____ = _____ Putts: _____ + _____ = _____

⑩ Par:
Score:
Yards:

⑪ Par:
Score:
Yards:

⑫ Par:
Score:
Yards:

⑬ Par:
Score:
Yards:

⑭ Par:
Score:
Yards:

⑮ Par:
Score:
Yards:

⑯ Par:
Score:
Yards:

⑰ Par:
Score:
Yards:

⑱ Par:
Score:
Yards:

CPSIA information can be obtained at www.ICGtesting.com
Printed in the USA
LVOW11s2001160913

352678LV00017B/1102/P